Fairy Tale Science

Making a Witch Trap for Hansel and Gretel

by Joanne Mattern

FOCUS
READERS®

BEACON

www.focusreaders.com

Focus Readers is distributed by North Star Editions:
sales@northstareditions.com | 888-417-0195

Produced for Focus Readers by Red Line Editorial.

Photographs ©: Chronicle/Alamy, cover (left), 1 (left); Red Line Editorial, cover (right), 1 (right), 11, 13, 15, 25; duncan1890/iStockphoto, 4, 29; Julia700702/Shutterstock Images, 7; Tim UR/Shutterstock Images, 8; Wildpix productions/Shutterstock Images, 16–17; djmilic/Shutterstock Images, 18; Charles Brutlag/Shutterstock Images, 21; Monkey Business Images/Shutterstock Images, 22; blambca/Shutterstock Images, 27

Library of Congress Cataloging-in-Publication Data
Names: Mattern, Joanne, 1963- author.
Title: Making a witch trap for Hansel and Gretel / by Joanne Mattern.
Description: Lake Elmo, MN : Focus Readers, 2020. | Series: Fairy tale
   science | Includes index. | Audience: Grades 4–6.
Identifiers: LCCN 2019033259 (print) | LCCN 2019033260 (ebook) | ISBN
   9781644930328 (hardcover) | ISBN 9781644931110 (paperback) | ISBN
   9781644932698 (pdf) | ISBN 9781644931905 (ebook)
Subjects: LCSH: Animal traps--Juvenile literature. | Hansel and Gretel
   (Tale)--Juvenile literature.
Classification: LCC SK283 .M333 2020 (print) | LCC SK283 (ebook) | DDC
   639/.1--dc23
LC record available at https://lccn.loc.gov/2019033259
LC ebook record available at https://lccn.loc.gov/2019033260

Printed in the United States of America
Mankato, MN
012020

About the Author

Joanne Mattern is the author of more than 200 books for children. Her favorite topics include science, history, biography, and sports. She also loves fairy tales and spooky stories. Mattern lives in New York State with her husband, children, and several pets.

Table of Contents

Chapter 1

Hansel and Gretel

Hansel and Gretel were lost in the woods. They were also very hungry. But soon they found a house made of candy. They began to eat. An old lady came out of the house. She invited them inside.

 At first, the old lady seemed kind to Hansel and Gretel.

Hansel and Gretel did not know it, but the woman was a witch. She used her house to lure children. Then she would cook and eat them.

Inside, the witch shoved Hansel into a cage. She told Gretel to build a fire in the oven. Gretel said she did not know how. The witch leaned into the oven to show her.

Quickly, Gretel shoved the witch inside and locked her in. Then she freed her brother from his cage. The children were able to escape.

 Hansel and Gretel needed to outsmart the witch to escape her home.

7

Chapter 2

Making a Witch Trap

Gretel had to think quickly to save her brother. She lured the witch into the oven. Then she trapped the witch inside. People in real life use traps, too. Most often, people catch animals in traps.

 In the fairy tale, the oven was the trap.

You can **design** your own trap. You can catch a stuffed animal. The trap should be big enough to hold your **target**. You should also have a way to close the trap around the target.

Materials

- Scissors
- 1 large cardboard box
- 1 long, sturdy stick
- 2 pieces of string, each 10 feet (3 m) long
- 1 stuffed animal

Instructions

1. With an adult's help, open the box and cut off the flaps.

2. Take one piece of string. Tie one end to the middle of the stick. Make a strong knot.

3. Take the second piece of string. Tie it around the stuffed animal.

4. Place the box on the ground with the open side facing down.

5. Use the stick to prop up the box. Place one end of the stick

Fun Fact

Live traps allow animals to be **released** back into the wild.

on the ground. Place the other
end of the stick against the
inside of the box.

6. Hold the loose end of the string that is attached to the stick. Move away from the stick until the string is almost **taut**. Keep holding the string.

7. Have a friend use the second string to pull the stuffed animal near the trap.

Fun Fact

Scientists trap animals to study them. They attach a **tracking** tag to each animal. Then they release the animals. They can see where the animals go.

8. Pull the string hard as the animal enters the trap.

The Wolves of Yellowstone

Gray wolves used to live in Yellowstone National Park. But by the 1970s, they were gone. During the 1990s, the US government trapped wolves in Canada. Scientists tagged the wolves with tracking collars. Then they released the wolves into Yellowstone. The wolves did well in their new home. Scientists tracked where they moved. They learned the wolves were starting new families. The project was a success. Trapping and tracking helped scientists **conserve** the wolves. In 2019, more than 60 wolves lived in Yellowstone.

Trapping helped scientists bring wolves back to Yellowstone.

Chapter 3

Results

When you pulled on the string, the stick fell. Without the stick to hold it up, the box also fell. It trapped the animal inside. You can adjust your trap to help it work even better.

 In this simple trap, the stick holds the box up until an animal comes close.

Try some of these ideas:

- Change the size of the box. It should be big enough to catch your target.

- Use a taller stick. This will create more room for the animal to enter the trap.

Fun Fact

Wild animals might bother people or pets. Never try to trap a wild animal. Only specially trained people should do this. They can trap animals safely. They can relocate the animals to safer places.

 Specially designed cages trap wild animals without hurting them.

- Change the strength of the string. Does it work better to use a thicker cord?

- Use a shorter or longer string. Does it work better to be closer or farther from the trap?

Chapter 4

The Science Behind the Trap

Your box trap works because of energy and **gravity**. Energy is the ability to do work. It cannot be created or destroyed. But it can change between different forms.

 Movement of any kind requires energy.

Potential energy is the energy of position. An object's potential energy is often related to gravity. This **force** pulls objects toward Earth's center. But gravity can be resisted.

For example, suppose a book is on a table. The book would fall if not for the table. The book has potential energy because of its position above the ground. Objects that are higher off the ground have greater potential energy.

POTENTIAL ENERGY AND GRAVITY

Potential energy is stored energy. It is the potential to move, not the movement itself. For example, gravity pulls on both balls. But the ball on the left could fall down. The ball on the right has nowhere else to go. So, the ball on the left has more potential energy.

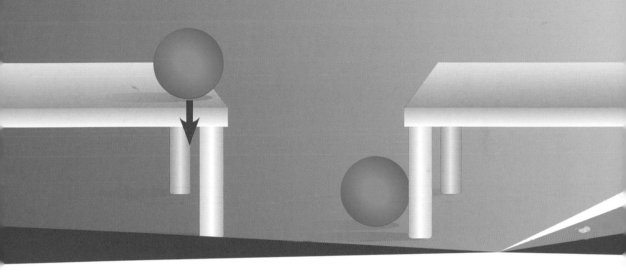

Imagine pushing the book off the table. The book falls. Its potential energy turns into **kinetic energy**. Kinetic energy is the energy of motion.

Energy changing between forms is what lets people make and use traps. When you first set up your box trap, it had a lot of potential energy. The stick held the box against the force of gravity. It kept the box from falling.

Fun Fact

Roller-coaster cars do not have engines. Instead, cars gain potential energy when they move up the first hill. Kinetic energy sends the cars zooming through the rest of the ride.

POTENTIAL ENERGY (PE) VS. KINETIC ENERGY (KE)

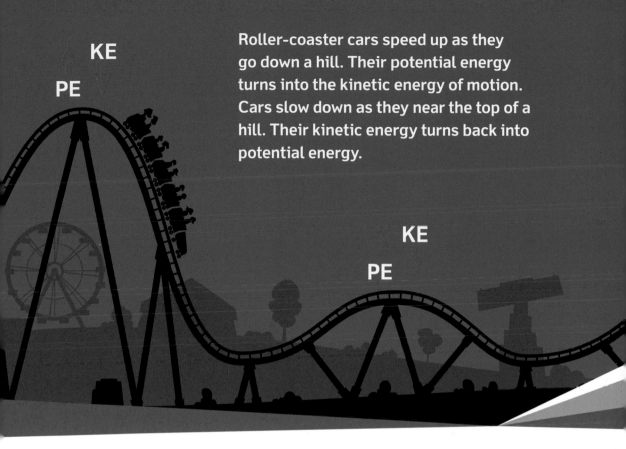

KE

PE

Roller-coaster cars speed up as they go down a hill. Their potential energy turns into the kinetic energy of motion. Cars slow down as they near the top of a hill. Their kinetic energy turns back into potential energy.

KE

PE

Then you pulled the stick away. The box fell. Its potential energy turned into kinetic energy. Gravity then kept the box on the ground. It trapped the stuffed animal inside.

FOCUS ON
Making a Witch Trap

Write your answers on a separate piece of paper.

1. Write a paragraph that summarizes the main ideas in Chapter 4.

2. Do you think trapping wild animals is good or bad? Why?

3. Why does the box fall when you pull the stick?
   - **A.** The kinetic energy of the box turns into potential energy.
   - **B.** The stick is no longer holding the box up against gravity.
   - **C.** The kinetic energy of the stick turns into potential energy.

4. What would happen if Earth had no gravity?
   - **A.** People would be pulled to the ground.
   - **B.** People would have no kinetic energy.
   - **C.** People would float away from Earth.

5. What does **lure** mean in this book?

*She used her house to **lure** children. Then she would cook and eat them.*

    A. to make people want to come closer
    B. to make people want to go away
    C. to feed someone candy

6. What does **relocate** mean in this book?

*They can trap animals safely. They can **relocate** the animals to safer places.*

    A. to move something to a new place
    B. to bring something in for study
    C. to identify an animal in
       a trap

Answer key on page 32.

Glossary

conserve
To protect something from harm.

design
To make a detailed plan for something before building it.

force
A push or pull that one object has on another.

gravity
The force one object has on another due to the mass of each object and how far apart they are.

kinetic energy
Energy that an object has because of its motion.

potential energy
Energy that an object has because of its position.

released
Let go.

target
A person or object chosen as the aim of an attack or trap.

taut
Pulled tight.

tracking
Following something to see where it goes.

To Learn More

BOOKS

Connors, Kathleen. *Forces and Motion*. New York: Gareth Stevens Publishing, 2019.

Felix, Rebecca. *Cool Engineering Projects: Fun & Creative Workshop Activities*. Minneapolis: Abdo Publishing, 2017.

Swanson, Jennifer. *Explore Forces and Motion!* White River Junction, VT: Nomad Press, 2016.

NOTE TO EDUCATORS

Visit **www.focusreaders.com** to find lesson plans, activities, links, and other resources related to this title.

Index

A
animals, 9–10, 12, 14–15, 19–20, 27

G
gravity, 23–27
gray wolves, 16

H
Hansel and Gretel, 5–6, 9

K
kinetic energy, 25–27

L
live traps, 12

P
potential energy, 24–27

S
scientists, 14, 16

T
tracking, 14, 16

W
witch, 6, 9

Y
Yellowstone National Park, 16

Answer Key: 1. Answers will vary; **2.** Answers will vary; **3.** B; **4.** C; **5.** A; **6.** A